THIS BOOK BELONGS TO:

♥

FOR ALL THE BEAUTIFUL
ANIMALS I'VE KNOWN,
AND ALL THE FRUIT
AND VEGGIES I'VE
GROWN...

BUT ALSO FOR MY
MUM AND DAD

♥

REBEL

Rebel Challenger

Rebel is an artist and wildlife carer who lives on a leafy acreage property surrounded by chickens and ducks.

As a working art director and graphic designer (and with a science degree from that time she dreamed of being a park ranger) Rebel uses none of these skills when drawing.

Instead, most of her artwork is inspired by the animals she cares for, the ones who visit her backyard and animals throughout the world she would love to meet one day.

Larrikin House

142-144 Frankston Dandenong Rd, Dandenong South Victoria 3175 Australia

www.larrikinhouse.com

First Published in Australia by Larrikin House 2021 (larrikinhouse.com)

Written by: Rebel Challenger
Illustrated by: Rebel Challenger
Cover Designed by: Rebel Challenger
Artwork & Production by: Mary Anastasiou (imaginecreative.com.au)

A CIP catalogue record for this book is available from the National Library of Australia. http://catalogue.nla.gov.au

ISBN: 9781922503374 (Hardback)
ISBN: 9781922503367 (Paperback)
ISBN: 9781922503350 (Big Book)

FORESTFRIENDLY
This book is printed on paper sourced from sustainable forests

NATIONAL
LIBRARY
OF AUSTRALIA

A catalogue record for this book is available from the National Library of Australia

FOOD OR FRIEND?

BY REBEL CHALLENGER

CABBAGE
BUTTERFLY

CRAB APPLE

DRAGON ♥ FRUIT

GOOSEBERRY

ALSO HONEY... BUT NOT A

BADGER

ALSO AN ICE CREAM CONE... BUT NOT A **WORM**

JELLY FISH

KIWI FRUIT

ALSO A LEMON...
BUT NOT A SHARK

MANDARIN
DUCK

ALSO A MANDARIN... BUT NOT A DUCK

ALSO AN OLIVE...
BUT NOT A
PYTHON

PINEAPPLE FiSH

ALSO A PINEAPPLE... BUT NOT A FISH

ALSO A PUMPKIN... BUT NOT A SPIDER

OUR FOODIE FRIENDS

JELLYFISH

These colourful marine animals are common throughout the world, often forming large groups known as blooms. Like the jelly you eat, jellyfish are wobbly, blobby-looking creatures. However, they also have long tentacles that when touched, can shoot out millions of tiny poisonous darts known as nematocysts, which can really leave a sting.

DRAGON FRUIT

Does a dragon fruit look like a dragon or does a dragon look like a dragon fruit? Either way, with their colourful skin covered in scaly spikes, these fruits of various cactus species from Central America look as enchanting as the magical flying dragons you read about in fairy tales.

CABBAGE BUTTERFLY

Also known as a cabbage moth. They don't look like cabbages, so why the name?
The cabbage butterfly lays its eggs on cabbage leaves and other vegetables. When the eggs hatch, hungry cabbage worms can quickly munch their way through an entire vegetable garden.

OLIVE PYTHON

The non-venomous olive python is among Australia's largest snakes. It is found in warm, rocky areas near water and can reach over four metres in length. This giant reptile ranges in colour from beige, to brown to the olive green it is named after.

GOOSEBERRY

The gooseberry is a small fruit. The goose is a large bird. They only seem to have their name in common. Some believe the 'goose' in gooseberry comes from old German, French or English words that changed over time to the current name.

TOMATO FROG

Hop over to Madagascar, east of Africa, to find the endangered tomato frog. These nocturnal amphibians range in colour from yellow through to red. If a tomato frog feels threatened, it will puff itself up to appear bigger... making it look a lot like a tomato.

PINEAPPLEFISH

Take a dip in Australia's coastal waters and you might see a pineapplefish. That is, if you swim at night. These small nocturnal fish hide during the day and move around after dark. With yellow scales and backward-pointing spines, it is easy to see how this fish got its name. It looks like a pineapple with eyes!

MANDARIN DUCK

No resemblance to the mandarin fruit. A more likely explanation for the name is that the colourful plumage of the male mandarin duck from East Asia reminded people of the ceremonial robes worn by important officials, known as Mandarin, in Chinese history.

PUMPKIN SPIDER

Once you see the female pumpkin spider, it's obvious where the name comes from. Her large orange abdomen looks like a miniature pumpkin! Pumpkin spiders are master web weavers, found mostly in parts of the Northern Hemisphere including Canada and Europe.

HONEY BADGER

Tough. Strong. Fierce. Honey badgers are not known for being sweet. But their tastebuds are. They eat insects, small animals and fruits, but their favourite treat is honey. Honey badgers are found in Africa, Asia and parts of India.

FIGBIRD

A medium-sized bird, with subspecies found in northern Australia and New Guinea. They don't look like figs, but they sure do like to eat them! Figbirds are mostly frugivorous (fruit-eating) but also eat insects. They live in open wooded areas and often like to visit suburban backyards

CRABAPPLE

A crab is a crustacean, a crabapple is a fruit. They have little in common except their name. Crabs are found in water and on land. Many walk sideways and are great to watch. Crabapples look like tiny apples and can taste sour... so maybe if you eat a raw one you might feel a bit crabby?

ICE CREAM CONE WORM

In shallow marine waters around the world, ice cream cone worms spend their time building shells to call home. The tiny shells are made of single grains of sand and other marine matter stuck together to create long tubes that end up looking just like miniature ice cream cones!

KIWIFRUIT

Kiwifruits are native to China and are also known as Chinese gooseberries. A long way away in New Zealand, the kiwi bird is unrelated. But you wouldn't think so. The flightless birds have brown, bristly, hair-like feathers & round bodies ... a lot like kiwifruits!

LEMON SHARK

We all know lemons can be sour so does that mean the lemon shark is too? Not at all. Lemon sharks are found in shallow subtropical waters and they must be fairly friendly because they often hang around in groups. Their name comes from subtle lemon-yellow colouring which is most obvious on their backs.